1,001 Facts Somebody Screwed Up

1,001 Facts Somebody Screwed Up

Deane Jordan

LONGSTREET PRESS
Atlanta, Georgia

Published by
LONGSTREET PRESS, INC.
A subsidiary of Cox Newspapers
A division of Cox Enterprises, Inc.
2140 Newmarket Parkway
Suite 118
Marietta, GA 30067

Printed in the United States of America

1st printing 1993

Library of Congress Catalog Card Number: 92-84015

ISBN 1-56352-064-8

This book was printed by Data Reproductions Corporation, Rochester Hills, Michigan.
Cover design by Karen Webster
Book design and typesetting by Kenneth Graham

If you know some "facts" that aren't true or need to be corrected, please send them to the author c/o Longstreet Press for volume 2.

To science, daughter of philosophy

Acknowledgments

I'd like to thank the following people, Mensans all, who helped in various ways with this book: Beth Anthony, Saul Cornell, Jim Halter, Mack Hill, Bill and Holly Horton, Lyn Larson Payne, Rick Obermeyer, Keith Proud, Phil Robertson, Brandon Shaw, Paul Synk, George Trepal, and one fellow Mensan who wishes to remain anonymous.

I would also like to thank the U.S. Postal Service, Eastern Kentucky University Library, the National Park Service, the Orlando Opera Company, the Florida Symphony, Opera America, the Maitland Public Library, Paul Schaefer, Ray Dawson, Don Burns—mechanic extraordinaire—world observer Barney Toth, buccaneer John Olden, Margery Tope, literary agent Joe Rhodes, and my parents, Robert H. and Mae Putney Jordan, who knew one day I would write something that wouldn't embarrass them . . . too much.

Introduction

If you ever go to Florida, you will notice that when it rains most of the drivers will turn on their headlights. If you ask them why, they will tell you that when your windshield wipers are on, you must have your headlights on, it's the law, everyone knows that. Well. . . . If you look up the headlight and windshield wiper laws, you will find it is not a law. That mis-notion started this book.

We are surrounded by distortions—intentional and unintentional—misinformation, things we are told or assume to be true. Journalists are always urged by their editors to "check it out"—even facts they know to be true, because checking it out is examining a fact from all angles. In this book we have walked around to the other side of hundreds of "facts." We have found many to be wrong in some way. Others we have looked at from new viewpoints, with interesting results. Considerable effort was expended to ensure their accuracy by cross checking with encyclopedias, standard references, and specialists. Occasionally, we did original research.

It is to the credit of our society that new techniques and investigations are constantly expanding and correcting incorrect knowledge. This is not revisionism, which is rewriting history to suit a particular viewpoint. This is simply getting down to the nitty-gritty.

Deane Jordan
Maitland, Florida

1,001 Facts Somebody Screwed Up

There are not exactly **1,001 facts** in this book. Some studious readers will count around 400; others will discern many more.

— ◆ —

Bulls can't see red. Like most animals, they're color blind. It is the movement of the cloth that urges them on.

— ◆ —

Searing meat does not seal in the juices. Yes, we know what your cookbook and your mother said. They're wrong. Sorry, Mom. Research shows that meat cooked slowly at lower temperatures is more moist than seared meat no matter how it is cooked after searing.

— ◆ —

In a real jungle you can't swing on **vines**. They're attached to the ground. Sorry, Tarzan.

Columbus's ships were not the Niña, the Pinta, and the Santa Maria. The Niña was actually the Santa Clare, the Santa Maria was La Galante. Pinta and Niña were nicknames given to the ships by their sailors. Santa Maria was that ship's official registered name. Pinta's official name has been lost to history.

There are only forty-six **states** in the United States. Virginia, Pennsylvania, Kentucky, and Massachusetts are commonwealths. Rhode Island, though a state, and the smallest at that, is actually the State of Rhode Island and Providence Plantations.

———◆———

Animal parents do not reject their **offspring** if humans handle them.

Charles Lindbergh was not the first to fly across the Atlantic Ocean nonstop. He was the first to do it alone. And there is serious doubt if Amelia Earhart did any flying when she became the first woman to fly across the Atlantic. Researchers say she was a poor pilot, and the two male pilots aboard did most or all of the flying.

———◆———

There is no evidence that **Betsy Ross** sewed the first U.S. flag. The story didn't even flutter forth from her relatives until 1870.

Artist Vincent van Gogh did not cut off his ear. Only a small portion of one lobe. Blame Hollywood if you believe otherwise.

Eskimos do not and did not live in igloos. Generally an igloo is an emergency shelter.

— ◆ —

Planting seeds by the full moon is no better than any other time. Experts tell us that this folklore is one of the most widespread bits of mis-information existing, and the hardest to change people's minds about.

"Elementary, my dear Watson," was never uttered by Sir Arthur Conan Doyle's Sherlock Holmes. Screenwriters should get the credit.

— ◆ —

The **tomato** is not a vegetable. It is a fruit, a large berry actually. (You probably knew that one.) The U.S. Supreme Court, however, ruled in 1893 that it was taxable as a vegetable because it is used like a vegetable. They earlier decided beans, although seeds, were also taxable as vegetables.

One does not get **tetanus** from a rusty nail. Tetanus, or lock-jaw, is a bacterial disease associated with manure-contaminated soil. It enters the body through any cut or bite. The rusty nail is only incidental. (We could tell you about the time our mother fell on a horse needle full of tetanus vaccine. Took the whole dose in the sit-down. Didn't hurt her one bit. Didn't get tetanus either.)

Emerson—Ralph Waldo—did not say, "Inconsistency is the hobgoblin of little minds." He said, "A foolish inconsistency is the hobgoblin of little minds." Big difference.

——◆——

Reportedly not all the **popes** have been male. Pope Joan supposedly dedicated several churches during her reign, 855 to 858. Many, however, deny her existence. It depends upon whom you ask. Male historians tend to say no, feminists tend to say yes.

Lucille Ball was not a natural redhead. She was a brunette in her first appearances.

Most black widow spiders do not, as a rule, eat their mates.

A cold does not turn into **pneumonia.** One is caused by a virus, the other bacteria.

—◆—

Household **appliances** do not really save you time. What time you save is used running other appliances and doing associated work. You spend about as much time in the kitchen doing chores as your great-grandmother did.

Nearly a dozen and a half well-controlled studies show **vitamin C** has no effect on preventing the common cold. Neither do antihistamines. Should add that there are more than 200 rhinoviruses, and you only get a particular cold once, thus as you age, you catch fewer colds. Ever wonder why we call it the "common cold"? Certainly there aren't "uncommon colds."

Brides do not walk down the church's aisle. They walk down the nave, which is the main area of the church from the principal entrance to where the clergy officiates. The aisles are up the sides.

Scholars are pretty sure Jesus was not born in the year 1 A.D. Four to six years earlier is more likely, maybe as many as twenty years earlier. What is at odds is not the event itself but some erroneous calculating centuries ago. Back then, birthdays were irrelevant. It was death dates that were recognized. Somehow that makes sense. That way you can judge someone's accomplishments and decide whether or not to recognize them.

Asia and Europe are not two **continents.** The ancients thought so because of the Bosporus straits, which connect the Black Sea and the Sea of Marmara. Mapmakers popularized the error. Bosporus means cattle crossing.

—◆—

Crickets do not chirp by rubbing their legs together. They rub their wings.

Camels do not have an unusually curved back-bone. In fact, they have some of the straightest backbones around. The illusion is caused by the hump, or humps, which are mostly fat.

Quicksand does not suck its victims down. In fact, one can float on quicksand. It is far more buoyant than water Quicksand, by the way, is not just a phenomenon of the tropics. To have quicksand, there must be a spring, a basin to catch the water, and enough sand suspended by the current to almost fill the basin. As long as the spring is running, the sand floats in the water causing quicksand. If the spring were to stop running, the sand would settle to the bottom, and not be quicksand.

Hair and fingernails do not grow after death. The flesh shrinks, giving that impression.

— ♦ —

Abraham Lincoln did not write the **Gettysburg Address** on the back of an envelope. In fact, he worked on the address for two weeks.

— ♦ —

The **dog days** of summer are not so named because Fido can't take the heat. It's because Sirius, the dog star, rises just before the sun in summer. The ancients thought that made the days hotter. Still, when we were growing up, we weren't allowed to play with our pooch during the dog days of summer.

The Statue of Liberty is in the territorial waters of New Jersey, not in New York. New York took political control of it, however, in 1834. Then the Feds took over. Ditto Ellis Island. Still, it is in New Jersey's waters.

Immaculate Conception refers not to Jesus' birth but rather to Mary's birth, which, theologically, was free from original sin. It did not become official church dogma until the 1800s, and then with some controversy.

Egyptians were not good **embalmers.** It was the dry climate that really helped.

—◆—

French fries did not originate in France, of that we're certain. Why call them French? Two possibilities. The story goes that French troops in Belgium during World War I liked the food so much that the Belgians began to call them French fries. The other explanation, which seems more feasible, is that anything cut into strips for cooking is called Frenched.

Elephants do not fear mice, or much of anything else. Should add they do not drink water through their trunk. They use their trunk like a straw, drawing water up into it, which they then spray into their mouths. Curiously, elephants form female-dominated social groups and are highly caring.

Plants do not grow toward the sun. In fact, the opposite is true. The sun reduces growth hormones on the sunny side of the plant, thus the plant actually grows on the non-sunny side, causing it to bend toward the sun.

——◆——

Precolonial America didn't have wild **boars** or **mustangs** roaming about. They were introduced by Europeans.

Only until recent times was north at the top of most maps. For several centuries of cartography, east was on top. Or shall we say, when the earth was flat, where the sun rose was the most important direction.

John F. Kennedy in his famous **Berlin Wall** speech didn't actually tell Berliners he was a jelly doughnut. His endearing linguistic slip misused an article, causing a very brief confusion between a pastry and an inhabitant of that city.

Catgut strings do not come from cats. Sheep are the source.

Moths are not attracted to flames, poets and lovers notwithstanding. The explanation is complex: In nature, moths navigate by light, usually the moon. They fly perpendicular to the natural light, at right angles to it, kind of like always keeping the moon on your right side. Since the moon is big, and they are small, there is no problem. They can't fly beyond the perpendicular influence of it. Along comes man with his tiny artificial lights that are nearby. The moth flies past your outside light, thinks it is the moon, then turns to keep it to one side, and turns and turns, slowly spiraling to the light. It is not attraction but rather ancient navigation thrown off by modern innovations.

There is no such thing as heat lightning, only lightning too far away to be heard by the observer, usually 17 to 20 miles.

The Colorado River did not create the **Grand Canyon**, technically speaking. Usually a river valley is created by the river eroding its way downward over time. In the case of the Grand Canyon, the plateau rose rather than the river cutting down. That explains how the east-to-west river manages to flow across a plateau that slopes north to south. One could argue that the river is about at the level it's always been. Further, the river had little to do with the width of the canyon, which was caused by rain, wind, temperature, and chemical erosion. And yes, to preempt the next question: the Grand Canyon is still growing.

Humphrey Bogart never said, "Play it again, Sam," in the movie **Casablanca,** or any other movie, sweetheart.

— ◆ —

Snakes are not slimy. They are quite dry, in fact.

> **There is no such thing as sea level since the ocean is always moving, everywhere.**

— ◆ —

Horses are not natural buckers. It's a tight strap around their genitals they're trying to buck off, not the rider. In fact, horses are quite gentle regarding people. You have little to fear in a horse stampede. Unlike cattle on the loose, horses will go around or over you if at all possible. Cattle will trample you, regardless. It's probably in their genes. Horses run to safety, bovines gore and trample.

Oriental **eyes** are not slanted. In fact, they are more horizontal than many Occidental eyes. It is the epicanthic fold that gives the tilted appearance—that and a low nose bridge. In the Orient, eyes that have long graceful curves, like those of a Siamese cat, are called Phoenix eyes.

———◆———

The **Mason-Dixon** line was not blazoned to separate slave and nonslave states.

Raccoons do not wash their food. It's an instinctive action from finding so much food in water. In a dry environment, the raccoon will still handle the food as if washing it.

It was to settle a boundary dispute in the 1760s between Maryland and Pennsylvania families.

Air isn't light, despite how it feels. It is pushing in on you with 10 to 20 tons of pressure. You don't feel it because you are pushing back.

— ◆ —

Stutterers don't always stutter. They cease to do so when singing and whispering. Incidentally, whispering is more wearing on your voice than shouting.

> **Wild Bill Hickock and ilk did not kill off the buffalo. The animals were bison. You have to go to Asia or Africa to find buffalo.**

— ◆ —

Historically, only Hawaiian men danced the **hula,** rather than all those lovely swiveling lasses we see in the movies.

— ◆ —

The majority of **bees,** 75 percent, do not live in a colony. They lead solitary lives.

Remember, you read it here first. Almost all the stories about people preparing for the end of the world as it approached 1000 A.D. are wrong. And no doubt as 2000 A.D. nears they will be dragged out of the fiction closet. Consider: Most reports of panic in 999 A.D. were written in the 1600s. There is no evidence or records from that time indicating any of the large-scale upheaval that the seventeenth- and eighteenth-century writers reported.

The popular notion that **Noah** took two of every living creature into the ark is not supported by biblical references. "Unclean" beasts, those that non-Jews like Noah could eat, were taken by twos; "clean" beasts,

Florida is not just an eastern state. Portions of it are farther west than Wisconsin. And while we're at it, Reno, Nevada, is further west than Los Angeles.

edible by the Hebrews, by sevens. That only covered a small portion of the animals around at the time.

——◆——

Flying **fish** do not fly. They glide.

——◆——

Most measuring **spoons** are not accurate but mass-market approximates.

Women do not have one more **rib** than men, but they do sometimes have one less tail vertebra. Men, however, do occasionally have more ribs than women.

— ◆ —

The **ostrich** does not stick its head in the sand.

— ◆ —

Bears don't truly **hibernate.** They just get cranky and sleepy.

— ◆ —

Clouds do not burst.

Lightning can and does strike twice in the same place. The belief otherwise comes from the notion that all lightning is sent by God as punishment. Should add that lightning strikes men about seven times more often than it does women. . . . Maybe it is from God.

Dogs do not sweat by panting. They sweat through their feet. The panting, however, does help cool them by an exchange of air.

Gumbo is not a culinary innovation of Louisiana. Sorry, y'all. That sticky, thick concoction has been around for a long time. Gumbo is the Bantu name for okra, which is also a West African word. Okra is native to Africa and is a member of the hibiscus family.

——◆——

Bluebeard did not exist. He is a folklore character. Blackbeard the Pirate did exist. Born Edward Teach, Blackbeard roved the waters of North America from Maine to the Gulf of Mexico. He supposedly died not telling anyone where his hidden treasure was.

America was not named for Amerigo Vespucci, although it has often been associated with his name. Modern thought is it came from the Spanish word Amerrique, which was from the American Indian word Americ, the name of a Nicaraguan mountain range, not far from where the first white man to approach the New World sailed. Further, usually an explorer's last name was used for naming a newly discovered place. Otherwise, we might have been stuck with Washington, D.C., as in the District of Chris.

The true height of Mount Everest is not known. Prior to the 1900s, six different heights were ascribed to it, from 28,990 to 29,026 feet. The average of those guesses was 29,000 feet, which looked like a pat guess, so it was arbitrarily changed to 29,002, some say 29,020. In the 1950s another team came up with 29,028, which is its height, for now. The problem is snow shift on the top.

Tomahawks were rarely thrown, despite what Hollywood says. And most serious fighters don't throw their knives either. Think about it. Would you throw away your only weapon?

Despite their names, **millipedes** never have a thousand legs. They can have from a couple dozen to several hundred but not a thousand.

———◆———

Those wrinkly **fingers** you get from washing the dishes are not caused by your skin shrinking. Fact is, the skin expands by absorbing water. How is this possible? Well, basic physics. Fresh water is not salty, the liquids in your body are. When different density solutions meet, they try to mix and distribute their collective elements equally. In this case the fresh water tries to dilute the solution through porous skin, thus waterlogging your finger tips.

Christopher Columbus was never known as such during his lifetime. He was Cristobal Colon. Should add that we really don't know what he looked like. The first painting of him was done years after he died, from memory.

—◆—

Xmas, meaning **Christmas**, has been around for centuries, possibly preceding the word Christmas. Also, it doesn't mean leaving Christ out of Christmas, as some accuse it. "X" is the Greek letter for Christ and was an important symbol of the early church.

> The suicide rate did not go up during the Great Depression. Nor are there more suicides during the holidays. In fact, many ill people near death manage to hold on until after the holidays.

You do not hear the ocean in sea shells.
You primarily hear echoes.

Sir Isaac Newton did not discover **gravity** while under an apple tree, nor did an apple hit him on the head, prompting a better idea. He did say, though, that while he was thinking about gravity he saw an apple fall. Gravity, as a scientific inquiry, was known in his time. He just applied it to places other than earth. Might we mention here that by most accounts Newton had a horrible personality and was quite vindictive.

Technically, **penicillin** does not kill bacteria. It keeps it from reproducing.

— ◆ —

No one is born allergic to **poison ivy** or **poison oak**. They acquire the allergy over time. Which means that he who brags he never gets it, will. Trust us. We had a case of poison ivy that was . . . enlightening. The ivy is more toxic in the spring and summer, and contaminated clothes can remain toxic for years. Lack of contact with the offending plant decreases sensitivity to the allergy.

> **The thumb is not a finger. Typically, then, you have eight fingers and two thumbs . . . unless pounding a nail, then it's all thumbs.**

Technically, a **moment** is not too brief. It's about ninety seconds. This might be a good time to mention that presently does not mean now. It means in a moment, soon.

—◆—

Despite common folklore, **opossums** cannot hang by their tails.

—◆—

> **The curve ball doesn't curve as much as it drops. Sliders, however, do curve.**

Moths do not eat cloth. Their larvae do. So why do we put stinky stuff in with our clothes? To keep ma and pa moth from setting up closetkeeping.

—◆—

There is no well-wrought statistical evidence to support the notion that there are more **homicides** during full moons.

Contrary to popular notions, Lucifer is mentioned only once in the Bible. And some argue it refers to the king of Babylonia instead of the devil.

Most **shark** attacks take place in shallow water, not deep water.

—◆—

Antiperspirants do not stop the body from sweating. They electrically short-circuit the process by which sweat is brought to the surface of the skin.

—◆—

Los Angeles is not the largest city in the United States. That distinction goes to Jacksonville, Florida, which is nearly twice the size of Los Angeles. L.A. is more populated, however.

—◆—

The **Japanese** did not fire the first shot at Pearl Harbor. The Americans attacked a submarine shortly before the planes arrived.

"Neither snow nor rain nor heat nor gloom of night stays these couriers from the swift completion of their appointed rounds," is not the motto of the **U.S. Post Office**, which has none. The familiar rubric is carved near the entrance of an old New York City Post Office. The motto is a corruption of an ancient comment on Persian post riders, similar to the pony express. The Persians were not deterred by "snow, or rain, or heat, or by the darkness of night."

> **Horses do not sleep standing up. They can take light naps on their feet, but they have to lay down for deep sleep. Some horses, it should be said, snooze standing up then crash over. Once down, horses will always get up front end first, the opposite of the way they go down (unless napping).**

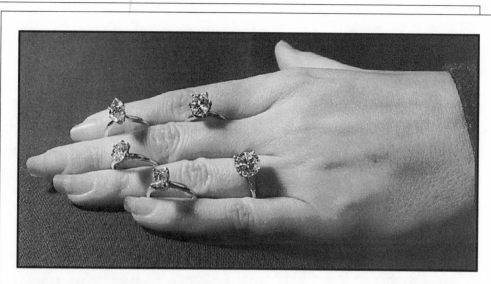

Diamonds haven't always been a girl's best friend. Only men wore diamonds until the mid-1400s. As the story goes, a French king's "lady" didn't like that, and fashion was forever changed. Which would explain why you have to have the wealth of a king to buy a diamond.

Nowhere in any of **James Cagney's** films did he say, "you dirty rat." Mimics say this line to represent the actor.

Humans are not the only animals that make tools. **Chimps** make skewers to impale termites, and chew leaves to make sponges to sop up water. Some birds use cactus spines to dig out insects.

—⸺ ◆ ⸺—

The **Wright brothers** did not invent airplanes nor powered flight. There is also reasonable evidence that they were not the first to fly in a plane. In fact, a U.S. congressman even introduced a bill to investigate their claim and determine whether one Dr. Samuel Langley had invented the heavier-than-air craft.

> **Scalping was more a European innovation than one practiced by American Indians. Further, only small portions of the scalp were usually taken (evidence of the attack). If the victim was alive at the time, it was usually not fatal. Blame Hollywood for the misconception.**

To "eat like a bird" is not to eat sparingly. **Birds** usually eat from one quarter to one half their body weight each day. Think about it.

—◆—

Dogs do not bark naturally. They learn it from other domestic dogs. Wild dogs don't bark. Growl, whine, and yip, yes, but not bark.

—◆—

Chain **letters** are not illegal. What is illegal is to threaten lives in such letters or solicit money, or so the post office tells us.

> **George Washington did not toss a dollar across the Potomac. Even if he did toss something, the dollar didn't come into being until after the United States gained independence, long after the fact.**

The **Puritans** were not antisex. They were for all things in moderation.

———◆———

Every year of a **dog's life** is not the equivalent of seven years in human terms. Best estimates now are that the first year is worth about 18 to 21 years, and each year thereafter four.

Research shows that one does not have to go to a prestigious college to get an excellent education. All things considered, the student's attitude is more important than the institution.

———◆———

There's little evidence to support the notion that **Robin Hood** ever lived.

Counting a **tree's rings** is not an exact way to determine a tree's age. During years of drought a tree may not add a ring, and in some seasons a tree, reacting to environmental traumas like pest attacks, will grow two rings.

— ◆ —

Crystal **goblets** are not crystal but glass. Ornaments were carved from crystal at one time, and making a glass that resembled crystal prompted the name to be picked up.

Bad breath is not caused by left-over food in the mouth, thus mouthwashes do little to control bad breath. It is what it says it is, bad breath, the body exhaling through the lungs elements of what you ate earlier. Bad breath caused by a bad mouth is a true medical problem.

The speed of sound is not set. **Mach one** at sea level at 32°F is 760 MPH. Go up seven miles and Mach one is 660 MPH because there is less air to carry the sound waves.

———◆———

General Grant was far from the first choice to lead the Union Army during the Civil War. President Lincoln first offered the job to West Point graduate Robert E. Lee. He had other plans.

You might have suspected this: Ants don't sleep. We've also read it would take 100 million ants to equal the weight of one horse. Thought you'd like to know.

Bulletproof glass is not. Successive rounds will go through it. All it does is buy those with good reflexes a little time.

The fate of the **Roanoke Island Colony**, the first in Virginia, is not so unknown. If you remember, the entire settlement disappeared leaving only the word CROATOAN carved in a tree. Travelers reported for decades later that nearby Indians had European features, such as blue eyes and red hair. The only question is whether the settlers were assimilated voluntarily via lack of food or by force.

The human skull is not one bone, but about twenty-two.

—◆—

This won't change your life, but it is true. Not all **manhole covers** are round. They also are made in squares and rectangles, but not triangles. The latter flip too easily. Now you know.

George Washington did not cut down the cherry tree. The story was borrowed and applied to him. Further, even if remotely true, the tree was not cut down, just hacked at.

—◆—

Pink for girls, **blue** for boys, isn't the way it's always been. Used to be reversed, and still is in some areas.

Sir Walter Raleigh did not lay down his cloak for his queen to walk on to keep her royal feet dry and clean. He also never made it to America. And despite a tobacco being named after him, he did not introduce it to Europe. He did advocate smoking, however, to support the tobacco trade.

California is in no danger of sliding into the Pacific. It will eventually slide into Canada. The continental plate it's sitting on is traveling north, not west.

You cannot sneeze with your eyes open.

We do not know if there are no two identical **snowflakes.** It is an assumption, nothing more. So let us assert here that there are indeed two snowflakes alike. Perhaps we can get a government grant to study this.

— ◆ —

Robert Louis Stevenson did not invent the story of Dr. Jekyll and Mr. Hyde. A real-life example existed at the time, William Brodie, deacon and thug.

Best guess is the center of the earth is not molten. It would be if it weren't under the pressure of everything above it. So it's hard molten rock, or something like that.

Most places that advertise an "Olympic-size" **swimming pool** are a bit shortsighted. To be Olympic-size, the pool would have to be fifty meters long, more than half the length of a football field.

The blind do not have better hearing than sighted people. They do, however, learn to listen more carefully. (Note: we never say the deaf have better eyesight.)

Alexander Graham Bell did not invent the telephone. He was using already invented items trying to make an instrument to help the deaf hear. He did, however, beat Elisha Gray to the patent office by only two hours, and thereupon mis-history turns. Gray sued and lost. Whether he was right or not, we'll never really know.

We can attest this one from personal experience: The building numbers on **Tokyo's streets** have no relation to each other and follow no practical order, should you ever visit there. The numbers come from the order of the building permits, meaning 10 can be on the east side of town, 11 on the west side. We got lost in Tokyo once, 1970 through 1972.

No Rockefeller had anything to do with the naming of Oysters Rockefeller. The entrée was green, like money, and the cook liked to name his creations after well-known people, or so the tale goes. And the facts are, you can't get original Oysters Rockefeller in this country. It used to be made with genuine absinthe, a narcotic.

Doughnut holes do not exist. Think about it. Philosophically (there has to be some philosophy in this book) the doughnut hole is a good example of the importance of language and thought and perception. The empty space in a doughnut middle is given a name, as if it were equal to the rest of the doughnut.

The **Greek Parthenon** was not destroyed by time. The occupying Turks stored gun powder there and it blew up in 1687.

—■◆■—

Uncle Sam did not have a beard until the beginning of the Civil War or so.

There never were any wild men of **Borneo,** at least not like the ones in circuses.

—◆—

The **heart** is not on the left side of the chest. It's about in the center with its strongest portion on the left side, thus, it can be heard slightly better from the left.

—◆—

Boards and bricks broken in karate demonstrations aren't necessarily regular boards and bricks. The boards can be heated to make them brittle and the bricks made with extra sand to make them weak. (Hint: Ask if you can provide the bricks and boards.)

There is no scientific proof that **subliminal** advertising or messages work. In fact, there is substantial proof to the contrary.

Got to trust the medicos on this one. They say a decapitated head is not aware of its surroundings or loss of body. Neurologically, decapitation results in instant unconsciousness, though the brain may take a few minutes to actually die. Reports from the French Revolution run counter to this, but things weren't too scientific back then. Writers of the day said heads tried to talk, smiled, laughed, grimaced, said prayers, rolled their eyes, and blinked at the crowd.

The famous little **Dutch boy** putting his finger in a dike to stop the flow never existed. The story was invented by American writer Mary Mapes Dodge in her book *Hans Brinker or the Silver Skates.* Reportedly, the Dutch got so tired of saying, "No, he doesn't exist," that they put up a statue to get tourist dollars.

Squirrels do not dig up the nuts they bury. Like a dog with its bones, they soon forget where they left them. They've got a good sense of smell, however, and dig up nuts other squirrels buried.

—◆—

Opossums do not "play dead." They actually faint. Should add there is a breed of goat that does the same thing.

Boiling water in an open pot is never hotter than 212 degrees, no matter how fast it boils. In other words, a **slow boil** and a **rolling boil** are the same temperature, but the rate of energy loss is different. Kind of like walking or running a mile— same amount of calories are expended. The difference is how fast the calories are burned up.

> **Alcohol does not help you sleep. In fact, just the opposite occurs.**

—— ◆ ——

That **crickets** can tell the temperature is not a wives' tale. Count the chirps in 14 seconds and add 32. You'll have the temperature in Fahrenheit. No, we didn't figure it out in Centigrade. But if you divide the number of chirps in 15 seconds by two you'd be close. Oh yes, only the male crickets chirp.

Theoretically, we are told, the **bumble bee** cannot fly, but no one has told the bee itself. This is one of those delicious tidbits that gets distorted. The key is energy. Early pundits decided the bee can't fly because of energy requirements they thought it could not meet. Well, the bee flies from gas station to gas station, so to speak. Bees can take off and land like a helicopter, and do so with a heavy load. Leads one to conclude that aerodynamics professors are flawed.

—◆—

Chickens don't sit on their eggs. They squat, keeping most of the body weight on their legs. We've reached under a sitting hen. Will wear leather gloves next time. . . .

Woody Allen is not Allen Stewart Konigsburg's real name.

Your dog won't see you in your fluorescent hunting outfit any more than the deer will—colorblind, you see. In fact, very few animals will see it except maybe your cat . . . and he couldn't care less.

Bats are not blind.

—◆—

Sap does not go up and down a tree depending upon the season, but rather inward and outward.

—◆—

Clarence Darrow, famous attorney and defense lawyer in the Scope's Evolution trial, never graduated from law school.

—◆—

A **mushroom cloud** can be produced by other means besides a nuclear explosion. Almost any large blast will produce such a cloud.

Bras did not always come in various cup sizes. The modern brassiere was invented by New York socialite Mary Jacobs, great-granddaughter of Robert Fulton. In 1914, Jacobs and her French maid sewed two silk handkerchiefs together and abandoned the whale-bone corset. Cup sizes did not come along until 1939. We're also told the majority of bra-wearing women wear the wrong size (now guess which way and we'll see if you're an optimist or a pessimist).

Cutting **hair** will not make it grow faster or thicker.

————— ◆ —————

The Puritans did not celebrate **Christmas.** They considered it a pagan holiday. It was illegal to celebrate Christmas in Massachusetts from 1659 to 1681. And kids went to school on Christmas in Massachusetts until 1870.

Cobras can't hear the snake charmer's piping. They follow the sway visually. In fact, no snake can hear. If it can hear, it is a legless lizard.

— ◆ —

Statistically, that barking **Doberman Pinscher** won't bite you nearly as often as a poodle. In fact, the smaller they get, the more apt they are to take a nip, kind of like a Napoleon Complex.

— ◆ —

There's no proof **dinosaurs** were green, or brown, or any color. Makes us muse about designer dinosaurs. You read it here first.

The science of fingerprinting was not developed for criminology but rather heredity studies. Further, fingerprints on documents have been used as identification since ancient times.

The infamous **Woodstock** Concert of 1969 was not held in Woodstock, New York. Although the concert was to be part of an arts festival there, it was actually held in Bethel, New York, several miles and a county away. Woodstock wouldn't allow the gathering. Bethel did, much to its regret. Poor Bethel, all of the headaches and none of the glory.

—— ◆ ——

Old West **wagon trains** formed circles when they stopped to camp to keep the animals in, not attackers out.

Frankenstein was the doctor, not the monster, in the original novel. The monster in this very interesting book is a far different creature than of late—quite literate and well spoken, in fact. He is persecuted for being strange, hunted when he has done no wrong. Where did Hollywood go astray. . . .

Ignoring for a moment those of us who believe the laws of probability are severely flawed (and thus drawing upon us the wrath of lower-level mathematicians)—the number of times you flip a coin has no bearing on the odds that the next toss will be heads or tails. According to traditional probability theory, every time it is a 50/50 situation, though most people will guess heads. A quiz: How many people do you need to invite to a party to have a 50/50 chance two guests will have a birthday on the same day? (ANSWER: Two. They either have a birthday on the same day, or they don't.)

Birds, such as the robin, do not listen for worms in the ground. They cock their heads to see better.

Karate did not originate in Japan but in Okinawa via China.

—◆—

There's no proof the Pilgrims ate **turkey** during their first and only Thanksgiving. Back then, turkey was a term used to describe any edible game bird.

—◆—

Not all **piranha** will strip your bones of flesh. Only four of the eighteen species are inclined to do so, and then only under certain conditions. The question is, which four?

—◆—

You're right. **Tiny Tim** was not that entertainer's name. He started out as Herbert Buckingham Khaury.

Toads will not give you warts, but some exotic ones do secrete poisons through their skins.

— ◆ —

Deer do not eat hay, and one of their favorite browsing snacks is poison ivy. For them it is a nutritious food, or so we've been told.

— ◆ —

Male mosquitoes do not bite. They're vegetarians.

Bagpipes did not originate in Scotland but rather the Middle East, probably Persia. They were introduced into Britain by the Romans. Northumbrian pipes, incidentally, are bagpipes filled by bellows instead of breath.

Fortune cookies were invented in the United States, not China. Add to that egg foo young, chow mein, and chop suey.

Branding cattle was not an invention of the Old West. Laws in New England approved it in the 1600s. There were eastern cowboys, too.

— ◆ —

Bullfighting was not a Spanish innovation. It is an ancient ritual that was practiced throughout the Middle East. The bull was one of the first gods of antiquity, and sacrificing him periodically was a big event.

Baseball was not invented in America. It comes from a British game called rounders. Basketball is home in the States, however.

—— ◆ ——

Teeth are not bone. Most references call them "hard substances," but they are simply teeth.

The Grimm brothers didn't write fairy tales. They collected them, then created fuller versions from the supposed fragmented ones they gathered from various German households.

—— ◆ ——

Hay fever isn't a fever and has little to do with hay. **Pollen** is the usual source of the problem.

—— ◆ ——

Trees do not leak **sap** on the hood of your car. That's from little insects up in the leaves using your automobile for a rest room.

Gas rationing during World War II was designed not so much to conserve gas but **rubber** and **tires.** Why? Because Japan had a near monopoly on natural rubber.

—— ◆ ——

Florida's **Everglades** is not a swamp but a very wide, shallow river flowing toward the Gulf of Mexico.

Johnny Appleseed is not a myth. His name was John Chapman and he did plant apple seeds. He was motivated by religious conscience to replace nature during a time when others were exploiting it. Chapman followed the teachings of Emanuel Swedenborg, founder of the New Jerusalem Church. Interesting man, Swedenborg,

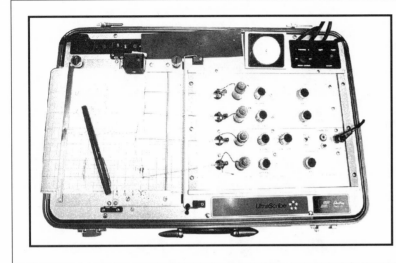

Lie detectors do not. Independent research consistently shows they are barely better than chance at detecting lies. That is why they are not admitted into a court of law unless both sides agree to it, and often not then.

The **funny bone** is not a bone but an exposed nerve.

—◆—

The toast did not originate to wish your guests health. **Toasting** was to demonstrate, by drinking first, that the wine was not poisoned.

Sardine is not a species of fish but a size of fish. At least twenty-one different kinds of fish can be sardines. By contrast, not all minnows are small fish. Minnows are members of the carp family, and one, the Indian Mahseers,

Nero never played the fiddle. It came along 1,500 years later. The best he could have done was pluck a lyre.

———◆———

Handel's Messiah was not written for a mega-chorus. It was written for about two dozen singers, or less.

———◆———

Most **plants** do not grow much in the daytime. They make food during the day, grow at night.

———◆———

Robert Fulton did not invent the steamboat. He improved the design.

Growing does not cause pain, physically at least.

— ◆ —

People don't start most forest fires. **Lightning** does.

— ◆ —

Despite press speculations otherwise, of this there is no doubt: The **Great Wall of China** cannot be seen from the moon.

— ◆ —

Walt Disney did not draw Mickey Mouse. The famous character comes from the pen of Disney's partner, Ubbe Ert Iwerks.

"Little Orphan Annie" was not the original name of that comic strip. In 1924 cartoonist Harold Gray thought up "Little Orphan Otto." The publisher he went to suggested a name change, and a skirt.

The stains on a smoker's fingers are not caused by tar. **Nicotine** turns brown when exposed to air, and its odor is what we identify as the smell of tobacco. Further, if one could consume all of the nicotine in a pack of cigarettes all at once—a drop or so—it would be lethal in fifteen minutes.

———◆———

Magellan did not sail around the world. He died part way, in the Philippines. The next fellow in charge, Juan Sebastian Del Cano, was the one who got the crew home safely.

There's little historical evidence to support the notion that pirates made victims walk the plank. Just heaved the poor sots overboard. They did keelhaul them, however.

There is no rule that says a **preposition** is something you can't end a sentence with. While it's a practice that has some roots in esoteric religious thought, there is no linguistic reason banning it.

— ◆ —

William Tell did not shoot an apple off his son's head. In fact, there's no evidence Tell ever existed.

Men do not have more **heart attacks** than women. They are at a greater risk earlier, but the heart attack rates for older men and post-menopausal women are about the same. Should add, contrary to popular belief, a man has a better chance of surviving a heart attack than a woman.

— ◆ —

Most **muggings** do not occur on back streets. The typical one is on the main drag.

Scientists are quite sure: Lightning travels from the ground up, not from the clouds down. An invisible stroke laces down and the visible one comes up to meet it, very quickly. So why does it appear the other way around? Best guess is the speed of lightning versus the speed of the eye to register the event, thus creating the illusion.

Dixie is apparently not a Southern term. Best guess is it originated with a musical in New York just before the Civil War.

Parachutes were around long before airplanes, in the 1700s in fact. They worked well with balloons.

The **Christmas tree** is pagan, not Christian. 'Tis said that Queen Victoria was the first to decorate a tree, but we doubt it. The Germans did so long before she did.

—◆—

Galileo didn't drop anything off the **Tower of Pisa**. A biographer made the story up.

Autumn leaves actually do not turn color. They lose one color, green, and show other colors they've had all along. The change is also caused more by the shortening of the days than by cooler weather.

Francis Scott Key did not write our **national anthem**. He penned the words then set them to an old English drinking song. Makes sense. Many people sound drunk when they sing "The Star Spangled Banner." It did not become our national anthem until 1931.

Air fresheners do not freshen the air. Most of them numb the nose instead. Thus your guests can smell the odors your anesthetized nose cannot. Don't believe us? Look up the ingredients on the can.

—◆—

Time to blame Hollywood again. Signing **X** for a signature started out not as a sign of illiteracy but piety. The X was for the cross and signified that the document was in order.

Dwarfs and midgets are not the same thing. Dwarfs have normal-size torsos but short arms and legs. Midgets are proportionally small all over.

The dinosaurs were not the largest mobile creatures on earth. The **blue whale** was and still is the biggest.

———◆———

Perspiration is odorless. It is bacteria on the skin that wafts offensively, or alluringly, depending upon the nose and the moment.

———◆———

Porcupines cannot throw their quills. Incidentally, they are rodents. And for those interested in such things, they are not born head first, needles pushed back, but the other way around—quite a thought. They do, however, come into this world in a sack, sparing mother porcupine considerable discomfort.

Most of the midnight ride of Paul Revere was accomplished by other horsemen. Joining him were William Dawes and Samuel Prescott. It was Prescott, in fact, who carried the warning to Concord, where the next day the first shots of the Revolutionary War were fired.

— ◆ —

Historians now tell us the Boston Tea Party was not to protest taxation but to steal the tea. (None of the bales were axed open for seawater contamination, but rather were tossed overboard for later retrieval.)

Chocolate does not cause acne, but it does have a chemical that helps counteract depression. Let's face it, chocolate is not just for breakfast anymore.

Flamingos are not usually pink. They are only pink in areas where there is a certain small mollusk in their diet. Get rid of the mollusk and flamingos are white.

———◆———

Mrs. O'Leary's cow didn't knock over a lantern starting the famous **Chicago Fire** in 1871. It was a colorful lie invented by a reporter, who later admitted it.

Experts say it is a coincidence and not intentional that the 46th word of the **46th psalm** of the King James Version of the Bible is Shake and the 46th word from the end is Spear and that the book was completed when Shakespeare was 46. (Don't count Selah at the end. It's a word for a symbol that means to pause.)

— ♦ —

Experts say there is no psychological harm in waking a sleepwalker.

The attack on **Pearl Harbor** was no surprise to Elliott Thorpe. A military attaché, he broke the Japanese code in Java and warned Washington of the pending attack several days ahead of time. The brass didn't take him seriously, ditto Dorothy Edgers, a Naval intelligence employee who decoded a message about the attack.

Woodpeckers don't get headaches, as best we can tell.

—◆—

No **witches** were burned at the stake in Salem, Massachusetts. Nineteen people were hanged and one crushed to death, but no burnings. The burnings were in Europe.

—◆—

You do not toss and turn in your **dreams.** One tosses and turns while one is not dreaming.

The swastika was not one of Hitler's designs. It was a common symbol in antiquity connected with sun worship. The tips of ancient swastikas, however, point counterclockwise; Hitler's version points clockwise. Interestingly, in Miami, Florida, there is a Swastika Park, named before World War II when the bent cross was a lucky sign. Efforts are underway to change the name.

Unicorns were not mythological, just European drawings done from the verbal descriptions of the rhinoceros. And until modern innovations, fanciful unicorns looked more like goats than horses.

No one is **double jointed**. Some people are just more flexible than others.

As a rule, St. Bernard dogs of old didn't carry casks of brandy. They were originally from Asia and used as rescue dogs at the hospice of St. Bernard in the Swiss Alps.

It was **Hercules,** not Atlas, who was condemned to hold the world forever upon his shoulders. Hercules then duped Atlas into the job. Or to put it another way, it's a handsome-dumb-jock story, Greek style.

——◆——

The **log cabin** is not an American innovation. The Finns and Swedes imported their technology and began building them in 1638 in Delaware.

——◆——

Lemmings don't drown en masse. In fact, they swim rather well.

Despite the appeal of such a thought, Henry David Thoreau was not a recluse. He didn't build his cabin by himself, spent only a couple of years there, and had a lot of visitors during the entire philosophic affair.

When **George Burns** and **Gracie Allen** started out, she was the "straight man" and he the cut up. Got more laughs the other way around so they changed their act.

It was not illegal to buy, possess, or drink alcohol during Prohibition. What was illegal was to make, sell, or transport it. One could also get whiskey with a prescription from a doctor. Should note cooking sherry came along about then, laced with salt so you couldn't drink it. And add that Prohibition brought about the birth of organized crime in the United States.

Male voices at **puberty** are not the only ones that change. Female voices shift downward also, but about a quarter the distance.

—◆—

Hitler was not German. He was Austrian by birth and was in fact kicked out of Germany in 1923 for his political activity. We should add that Hitler was not illegitimate.

The **Declaration of Independence** was not approved on July 4, 1776. Only John Hancock, for the assembly, signed it that day. The other signatures came later, August 2. And one could argue that July 2 is really Independence Day, for that is the day it was declared.

The Emancipation Proclamation freed no one. It did, however, promise freedom to slaves in the rebelling southern states, but not in the northern states.

——◆——

The research is conclusive: Swimming shortly after eating will not cause **cramps.**

It was **diseases** from Europe, not wars, that killed most of the Indians in the Americas.

—◆—

Alcohol doesn't warm you. That's just an illusion. In fact, it helps cool you off, internally or externally.

—◆—

Fish do not drink, so if you drank like one, you'd be dead.

Pigs are not dirty. Given a choice, a pig will live a very clean life. And since they do not have sweat glands, they do like to wade in cool, clear water. Pigs also are among the smartest of all the animals. Add the octopus on that bright list. Squid, on the other hand, are quite stupid.

Technically, the **earth** is not round. Kind of flat near the top.

You've got a left foot and a right foot, correct? And you have a left shoe and a right shoe. A couple of hundred years ago, there were no left and right shoes, just footwear, all made the same.

A **compass** does not point to true north but magnetic north, several degrees off to the west.

A **peanut** is not a nut but a legume. To be a nut, it would have to grow above ground. The peanut grows in a pod below ground. Interestingly, the peanut is a native of South America. Sailors carried it from there to Africa. African slaves then carried it to the southern plantations where peanuts were considered good for only pigs and slaves to eat. It remained an ignored plant until the Civil War, whereupon its oil became valuable. Incidentally, the African word for peanut was nguba, from which we get goober, the nickname for a peanut.

Jamestown, Virginia, was not the first colony in the New World. After Chris Columbus lost a ship in 1492, he left a few dozen of his men in the Caribbean when he sailed back. The natives had killed them all by the time Chris returned. Seems the sailors were very poor neighbors.

Chicago is not a windy city. It is not in the top ten windy cities of the United States. The term supposedly evolved from the propensity of its politicians to talk at length. Should add that Chicago is an English version of an Algonquian word meaning "place of the wild onion."

Oysters can be eaten any month. The prohibition about eating them only during months that have an r in their name is an outgrowth of the time before refrigeration, when spoilage was common.

George Washington wasn't the first U.S. president. **John Hanson** was president of the Congress of the Confederation and carried the title of president of the United States, as did eight men after him. George was number nine, after the arguments settled.

— ◆ —

The atomic bomb dropped on Hiroshima during World War II was not the most fatal attack of the war. Up to 80,000 people were killed in that blast. The conventional bombing of Dresden, Germany, killed upward of 135,000, and an earlier firebomb attack on Tokyo killed 145,000.

Cinderella wasn't supposed to wear glass slippers. Translator Charles Perrault mistook pantouffles en vair, or squirrel fur slippers, for pantouffles en verre—glass slippers.

The **golf tee** did not become official until 1922. Before that, golfers whacked the orb off a small pile of wet sand. The tee was patented in 1899.

—— ◆ ——

Beavers do not carry mud on their tail, or use their tail as a trowel.

—— ◆ ——

A drowning person does not surface three times. That is an old notion associated with the **Holy Trinity**. Same thing with the superstition that lighting three things with one match is bad luck.

Possession is not nine-tenths of the law. Possession is not the same thing as ownership, and if someone else owns what you possess, it is his, not yours, and you are in trouble.

Beavers do not build dams that curve against the flow nor can they drop a tree where they want it. They're also not too bright. Sometimes they are killed by the trees they gnaw down . . . one might call it chewicide.

— ◆ —

Halley did not discover the comet named after him. It had been seen more than a dozen times before he saw it. **Halley,** however, did accurately predict its return in 1758.

— ◆ —

The **Bible** does not say, "God helps those who help themselves."

Pandora's box that most Greeks speak of wasn't really a box but a jar. And it contained not the vexes of humanity but virtues for her wedding presents, all of which flew out to the people when she opened it, except hope, which stayed to console her.

An **arm** or a **leg** does not "fall asleep," nor has blood circulation been cut off from it. Just a major nerve has been irritated by pressure.

—◆—

Worldwide, black is not the most common **mourning color.** White is, and has been for centuries.

Coffee beans are not beans, but the pits of a fruit that resemble beans. They get about one pound of "beans" per year per evergreen tree.

Just because a trademark is protected does not mean it cannot lose its status and become a generic name, as these trademarks have: kerosene, corn flakes, yo-yo, mimeograph, shredded wheat, and nylon. Xerox, for example, is a company that judiciously protects its trademark and would be upset if you told someone to "xerox this page." In their way of thinking that's like saying "Frigidaire the beer."

Raindrops aren't shaped like tears. They're flattish, more like a hockey puck than a tennis ball.

———◆———

The **Statue of Liberty** is not that monument's name. It is Liberty Enlightening the World.

Thomas Edison did not invent the electric light bulb. History gives credit to Sir Humphrey Davy in 1802. Edison's employees found a long-lasting filament making it commercially feasible. When he said genius was 99 percent perspiration and 1 percent inspiration, he was talking about other people's sweat and genius. It was the phenomenal genius Nikola Tesla whose theory of electricity lights the world, not Edison's. Tesla was seminal in electricity, computers, microwaves, robots, nuclear fusion, and missiles. Pitifully poor, he tried to sell his patents to Edison, but the Ego of Menlo Park would have nothing to do with his superior. George Westinghouse bought them instead.

Well-known home economist Betty Crocker never existed. She was invented by a PR man in the 1920s. Should add no Betty Crocker has ever been seen from the waist down. Unlike Betty Crocker, Aunt Jemima was a real person.

Nonfunctioning **buttons** on men's suit coats are not for decoration. They're adopted from old German uniforms that used buttons to keep the wearer from using the sleeve to wipe his nose. Tell that to your five-year-old.

———◆———

Birds don't fly by flapping their wings up and down. **Bird wings** move more forward and backward, like a figure eight on its side, if viewed in very slow motion. Honeybees fly the same way.

There are no **antelopes** playing on any range in North America.

—◆—

Casanova did not have any special charm over women. He said he simply knew which ones to ask. It should be noted that he also ran out of sexual steam by mid-life.

—◆—

December 25 was not set as the date for **Christmas** until 354 A.D.

There is no proof that the Pilgrims in 1620 stepped on the rock now enshrined at Plymouth, Massachusetts. The story wasn't mentioned until 1741, by a Pilgrim descendant who was born twenty-six years after the purported event.

Indians didn't get their hands on General George Armstrong Custer's famous long hair after the **Battle of Little Big Horn.** Custer got a hair cut just before riding out.

Most people who say they are **tone deaf** are not. A tone deaf person speaks in a flat monotone. Most people who say they are tone deaf simply have not developed beyond childhood skills in matching pitches. Same thing happens with drawing skills, and dance.

—◆—

Contrary to myth and television specials, **toads** cannot live for years inside rock. One year is about the best they can do without food or water. What scientists think happens is that young toads crawl into holes, grow too large to get out, and are then discovered there by people, who believe they were entombed there eons ago.

Ketchup is not an all-American condiment. It was originally a Chinese medicine.

There is no set time a person must be missing before he or she is declared legally **dead.** In fact, heirs have to go to court in most jurisdictions to request such a ruling. Usually they have to prove the person in question has indeed been missing.

When you snap your fingers, it is not the thumb and finger separating that makes the noise but the finger slapping against the heel of the thumb. Don't believe us, huh? Hold a dollar bill on the heel of your thumb and try to make a snap. See, can't be done. Now that you've lost the bet, send the dollar to the author at. . . .

Not all doctors take the **Hippocratic Oath.** In fact, very few do, and those who do take an oath take a significantly different one from the original. Older doctors who took the oath pledged to lead a life above reproach. Further, the original Hippocratic Oath was probably not written by Hippocrates.

Henry Ford did not invent the automobile. Gottlieb Daimler in Germany beat him by about eighteen years in 1890, as did Karl Benz. Daimler named the car after his distributor's daughter. You may have heard of her, Mercedes. Later they got together.

As birds go, the owl is quite stupid and certainly not wise. Crows are said to be the brightest, blue jays close behind. Had a blue jay for a pet. She had an amazing array of sounds, and an exceedingly independent attitude.

Four-leaf **clovers** are no longer rare.

———◆———

Suits of **armor** were not heavy and cumbersome. Only jousting suits of armor were weighty. The ones used for fighting were quite light. Why do we think they were all heavy? That's what museums usually display. Why display those? you ask. Because they last longer, perhaps.

———◆———

Children are not naturally afraid of the **dark.** They simply come to associate darkness with being left alone, which they do not like.

Frontiersman **Daniel Boone** disliked coonskin hats, probably never wore one. In fact, he was rarely depicted with one until television came along.

Lost people do not wander in a **circle** because one leg is stronger or shorter than the other. Seems circling is an innate response. It is the straight line that is unnatural.

Tall buildings do not sway in the breeze, or so engineers tell us. Somehow our stomach doubts that.

More people attend professional opera performances than attend pro football games. Should add most football fans watch the game on TV, whereas opera is best live. In addition, two million people a month attend symphony concerts in the United States. Most sports fall shy of that as well. Then why, one should ask, do professional sports seem more "popular" than the arts? Several reasons. TV and advertising are two of them. But overall, ticket buyers spend about twice as much money on the arts than on sports.

"Don't count your chickens before they hatch" is not a new saying. **Aesop** said it around 560 B.C.

Lassie was never female. A series of male dogs played the part, in drag so to speak.

——◆——

Before you label **chopsticks** an inferior way to eat food, consider that Orientals do not think so. They used to eat with metal utensils, specifically the knife. Chopsticks, in their way of thinking, elevated man to a more civilized plane. One of the scourges of old age in the Orient is being forced by infirmity to eat with a fork or spoon.

——◆——

Blood is thicker than water, but barely, almost not enough to count.

If you went out in your backyard in the United States and dug through the center of the earth, you would not come up in China. More like the Indian Ocean, somewhere near Australia.

The shortest distance between two points isn't necessarily a **straight line**. On a sphere, a curved line can be shorter, such as flying near Greenland when traveling from Paris to New York.

The majority of the world's oil does not come from the Middle East. Did we mention that oil from the ground is actually dark green, rather than black?

The famous picture of Marines raising the flag over **Iwo Jima** was staged to replicate the original raising earlier.

The temperature and dryness of a **dog's nose** have nothing to do with the canine's health.

———◆———

It was Cicero, not President **John Kennedy**, who first said words to the effect of, "Ask not what your country can do for you, but what you can do for your country." Supreme Court justice Oliver Wendell Holmes also expressed similar sentiments.

———◆———

Sex, or lack thereof, does not cause acne.

The famous painting of Washington crossing the Delaware, standing proudly in the front of a small boat with ice floes around, is woefully inaccurate. First of all, the flag displayed behind George didn't come into being until at least a year after the crossing. Other problems are: the boats are too small for their type; soldiers of that period never held their gun barrels up because snow and rain would dampen their gun powder; and the fact that George was probably smart enough not to stand up in a boat, let alone make a target of himself, speaks eloquently. The picture was painted way after the fact, in Germany.

Identical twins are not identical. They only appear to be if you don't look too closely. They have different fingerprints, for example.

———◆———

Birds do not sing because they are happy. It is a territorial behavior.

———◆———

Exercise does not increase the **appetite.** Got to find some other excuse to put on the pounds.

———◆———

You do not have any more freckles now than when you came of legal age, or so say the medicos.

President Theodore **Roosevelt,** despite the press, hated the nickname "Teddy." His last words, incidentally, were "put out the light."

There is no evidence—nor contemporary accounts—to suggest that Lady Godiva ever rode naked through the byways of Coventry, England. Peeping Tom, while more believable perhaps, is also as fictitious. Accounts date from decades after the purported event.

Generally speaking, the **brain** has no feelings. Headaches are caused by problems with nerves, muscles, and other tissue on the outside of the skull.

—◆—

Whole milk is not good for an **ulcer.** The fat content eventually irritates it. Skim milk is far better.

—◆—

Saltpeter, or potassium nitrate, does not reduce male sexual desire. In fact, potassium nitrate is a common preservative.

Bats do not get caught in people's hair.

———◆———

Contrary to some thoughts, the **bubonic plague** still exists. The United States had a bout with it around 1900, and about 10,000 people died from it in the 1960s and 1970s in Vietnam.

The "pharaoh's curse" associated with the opening of King Tut's tomb in the 1920s did not manifest itself, despite sensational stories and TV shows to the contrary. The majority of the workers who opened the tomb lived to ripe old ages.

Not all ripe **oranges** are orange. Some can be green. Further, unlike other fruits, oranges can only ripen on the tree. If anyone advertises "tree-ripened oranges" then it is empty advertising.

——◆——

The **bikini** was not "discovered" on natives in the South Seas. It's been around since at least the Roman days.

Gravity is not the same throughout the world. It tugs at different intensities in different places, depending upon the subsurface density. The gravity is measurably stronger in Hawaii, for example, than in Maine. Colorado is very light, comparatively speaking. In fact, oil exploration depends upon favorable gravitational measurements.

The **White House** in Washington wasn't always white. It was gray until after the War of 1812, when it was rebuilt and painted. The building was remodeled in 1902, when it officially became the White House.

——◆——

Proponents would be hard pressed to find a case of human **spontaneous combustion** that cannot be reasonably explained.

Girls do not naturally throw a ball "like a girl." Lack of practice is the key. For the most part, girls can throw well, as many boys do, if they spend considerable time at it. Put a ball in a boy's nondominant hand, and he'll throw "like a girl."

Hot debate: Some scholars believe **Andrew Jackson** was born at sea in 1755, not 1767, and thus was not eligible to be president of the United States, a somewhat moot point. However, to this day at least two states, North Carolina and South Carolina, claim his birth place, about a mile apart.

Worms are not the preferred food of fish. Aren't too many earthworms in water for fish to be used to them.

— ◆ —

The **sweet potato** and the **yam** are not the same vegetable. Two different plants altogether. In fact, a relative of the yam provided the first hormones for birth control pills. Some theorize the Aztecs ate this vegetable in times of famine and thus reduced their population, unintentionally.

Walking on hot coals is not the feat it is made out to be. One should know such public coal-walking is done when the coals are quite burned down and well coated with ash (and after dark so they look more menacing than they are). Like running a finger through a flame, a short exposure is not harmful. It's hanging around to discuss the weather that will get you burned. (No, we are not accepting any challenges. Let the physicists do that. We logicians know better.)

Truth serum does not work. Sorry Hollywood. Primarily an anesthetic, truth serum is sometimes a hypnotic. It renders you unconscious rather than a babbling traitor.

Sorry, Popeye—spinach is not high in iron. In fact, it has next to the lowest amount of all vegetables. The story is that a government publication misplaced a decimal point, thus creating the impression way back that spinach is rife with iron. The only vegetable with less iron is the cucumber, with .1 mg. per serving. Spinach has .2 mg., tied with celery. On top? Dandelion greens, with 5.5 mg. per serving, followed by soy beans, 5.4 mg.

William Faulkner is not that writer's name. For at least
two generations it had
been Falkner. The story
goes that the fellow
who printed William's
first book made a mis-
take on the title page,
prompting him to
change to Faulkner.

—◆—

Mona Lisa's lack of
eyebrows is not abnor-
mal. Was fashionable
then.

Fifty percent chance of **rain** doesn't mean that half the area will get rain. What it means is that during the last 100 days with the same meteorological conditions it rained 50 out of the 100 days.

—— ◆ ——

Despite the hype, **killer bees** are not much more of a threat than other bees. They are quicker to swarm and attack, but

Dracula is not a myth, so to speak. He arose as the central character in a novel of that title in 1897. The character was patterned after Vlad IV, the Impaler, a fifteenth-century Walachian prince.

interbreeding could dampen that as they move northward. Domestic bees and hornets are far more of a threat at the time being.

People who say they do not dream simply don't remember their dreams. Research shows everybody **dreams,** several hours a night.

—–◆–—

Antarctica is not just a pile of ice and snow. There is a land mass under all that frigid landscape. The North Pole, however, just floats.

—–◆–—

Bones are not white, dry things, except outside the body. When alive they are tan and quite full of marrow and blood.

Fright does not turn one's hair white. In fact, gray hair is not a color but an absence of color pigments in the hair. Furthermore, hair does not turn gray overnight.

The **Liberty Bell** was not made in the United States. It was cast in London in 1752. It was not rung on the first Fourth of July and actually cracked in 1835. Should also add it was not called the Liberty Bell until the 1830s, and not after the colonists but rather for slaves seeking their freedom.

> **The sun isn't round. Flattened on top and bottom.**

Television and movies aside, one cannot introduce a "new" **witness** in a trial and have a Perry Mason ending. Simply isn't allowed. In most states, both sides have access to the same information and witnesses. The battle plan is how to control and present the evidence and witnesses to the jury. Surprise witnesses or evidence is cause for mistrial in most states. Sorry, TV.

In Shakespeare's *Julius Caesar*, **Brutus** says he hears a clock strike. Cassius says it struck three. The problem is there were no clocks in Caesar's day. Hourglasses and sundials kept time back then. Incidentally, the way a shadow moves around a sundial—clockwise—influenced the direction hands move around a clock.

—◆—

"Yankee Doodle" is not an American song. It was a British ditty designed to harass ragtag colonists during the French and Indian War. Incidentally, the macaroni mentioned in the song is a reference to an eighteenth-century dandy, not the pasta.

Breast feeding does not always prevent pregnancy, but it may raise the IQ of the child, according to at least one study.

Most fireplaces are not a good source of heat. They actually remove warm air from a room because they need air to burn. Now, if you provide outside air for the inside fire to burn, the operation becomes far more efficient.

The **Sabbath** and Sunday, the Lord's Day, are not the same. In the commandments, the seventh day of the week, Saturday, is called the Sabbath. Early Christians adopted Sunday, the first day of the week, as their day of worship, a change that is still reflected in our calendars.

Mosquito **repellents** don't repel. They hide you, so to speak. The spray blocks the mosquito's sensors so the little varmints don't know you're there.

——◆——

Humans are not the only creatures that wage **war.** Ants do so, and they take slaves as well.

——◆——

Albert Einstein did not make bad grades. He studied at a university at a time when getting in was tough. Actually, he got good grades. The school had a system of grading where 1 was the highest. Then it changed its system so that 4 became the highest. Albert got 4's, and researchers thought 1 was good, 4 bad, thus the rumor.

Caffeine is not a stimulant. It blocks body regulators, and your own body revs you up.

London Bridge is not in London. It was moved to Arizona, where it now spans the Little Thames River, a short canal off the Colorado River.

Florence Nightingale didn't do much nursing. In fact, only about three years of her life at the most was spent nursing, primarily during the Crimean War, 1854-56. She was, however, quite an administrator and innovator and therein her fame rests. She started nursing schools and organized medical organizations. We also should relate a most interesting fact: She spent the last forty years of her life in one room, never leaving, although there was no stated reason for doing so.

Fish are not immune from sea sickness.

—◆—

The **brain** of modern man is not as large as the brain of a Neanderthal.

—◆—

Your **bones** aren't the toughest substance in your body. Teeth enamel takes first place.

—◆—

According to experts, most self-help **books** don't help.

Attorneys and lawyers are not the same thing. Lawyers graduate from law school. Only they can call themselves lawyers. An attorney, however, is anyone authorized by you to act on your behalf. Your best friend can be your attorney. That's why they call various documents power of attorney. An attorney-at-law is usually a lawyer who acts on your behalf regarding all legal proceedings.

We're going to go out on a limb on this one: The **sky** is not blue. Yes, if you look up it appears blue. But, the sky is actually black, as astronauts can attest. The blue is caused by light reflecting off bits of dust and moisture in the atmosphere. A combination of what is and is not reflected creates our sensation of color. Technically the sky looks blue to our eyes because that is the one color that is not reflected. So, the sky is every color except blue. (If we keep writing like this, it may be time to run for political office.)

> **Astronauts are not weightless while orbiting the earth. They are, in effect, in constant free fall. If the space shuttle were to stop its forward motion, it would drop, quite heavily. But its thrust carries it forward while gravity tugs down at it, keeping it from shooting out into space.**

Britain's King George V did not die naturally, as the world thought at the time. Contemporary historians say that in 1936 George was indeed hours from death. The family had already consented to a nice and tidy end to the monarch's life. Arrangements had been made, but George, in a coma, wasn't dying on time. His physician, Lord Dawson, realized that George was going to fatally abdicate after the *Times*, of London, went to press. That meant George's demise would be announced first in the evening newspapers, which at the time were not good enough for royalty. So Dawson told the *Times* by message to push back their deadline and wait. With the royal family out of the room and only a nurse for a witness, Dawson—who recorded his actions—injected George with morphine then cocaine, bringing a swift and peaceful end to the monarch. Talk about a deadline. . . .

Shouting at stinging **honeybees** won't help. They can't hear. Don't have any ears. Ditto snakes.

—◆—

The first printed book was not the **Gutenberg Bible**, unless you restrict the competition to Europe. The Chinese were printing with moveable type centuries earlier. Diamonds are not indestructible. They crush easily and burn.

Footballs are not, and never were, made of pigskin.

Using Navajo Indians and their language during World War II to stump Japanese **code breakers** was a brilliant stroke. Unfortunately, it was not an original idea. During World War I, German code breakers in Europe were thwarted by Americans using Choctaw Indians to relay orders.

The **Arctic** is not always cold. Summer temperatures in the Arctic Circle can reach 90°F, and a variety of crops can be grown.

—◆—

Coffee beans are not naturally flavorful. They are void of taste until roasted. Should add that **coffee** was originally cultivated in the Middle East, not South America. In fact, it was used to make wine for centuries. Coffee as we know it evolved in the thirteenth century. The trees didn't get to the New World until the early 1700s.

Despite what the media portrays, cavemen and dinosaurs never saw each other. Lived in different times.

—◆—

Vampire bats do not suck blood. They bite, then lick up the flow.

Most transsexuals who go from female to male do not have surgery to make them appear physically complete. Most only appear male by the clothes and hairstyles they wear. Males who become females, however, usually go all the way.

The notion of buxom **Amazons** is not mythologically correct. Amazon means breastless ones. The ancients Greeks believed Amazons removed their right breasts so they could handle bows better.

—◆—

Touchy subject: **Football** is not the professional sport that draws the greatest number of spectators. Baseball is more than three times as popular. In fact, college football outdraws professional football by more than 2 to 1.

Cats do not always land on their feet. They try to but don't always succeed.

It is not illegal in most places to use a name other than your own as long as there is no intent to **defraud** or **deceive.**

---◆---

The **eyes** in certain portraits do not follow the observer, nor is it a trick. It is a matter of perception. If the eyes are situated so they look exactly straight forward, they will appear to follow the viewer. The TV screen produces the same effect.

Despite reports otherwise, Hitler did not snub the great black athlete Jesse Owens when he won four gold medals in the 1936 Olympics. Owens himself said he was not snubbed. He reported that when he passed Hitler, the German leader rose to his feet and waved. Owens said he waved back. Further, Owens was critical of writers who said Hitler snubbed him.

Lions are not kings of the jungle. Lions do not inhabit jungles. Can't run in the jungle. They like the plains where they can run down game. Sorry, Tarzan.

—◆—

The first **baseball** game telecast was not in the United States but Tokyo.

There are not five **senses,** nor are there six. A more accurate number is around twelve, depending upon definition. Traditional wisdom says there are five: sight, hearing, taste, touch, and smell; some add ESP as a sixth sense, though research to support that notion is wanting. Factually, we perceive things that are not accounted for by the traditional list. The list now incudes the sense of balance, temperature, pain, a sense of muscles, and our internal organs.

The world's best-selling video, as of early 1992, was not of a rock group or a movie but of the world's three greatest tenors in concert, Luciano Pavarotti, Placido Domingo, and José Carreras at the World Cup concert in Rome.

The **Pilgrims** and the **Puritans** of early Massachusetts were not the same people, although encyclopedias, artists, and journalists mix them up all the time. It is not at all unusual to see Thanksgiving posters showing Puritans instead of Pilgrims. The Pilgrims, as a rule, did not wear big silver buckles on their belts and hats, and the women were not always bonneted with dainty white caps. In fact, their clothes were a mish mash and often garish. It was the Puritans who were somber in habit and dress.

> **Not all swiss cheese has holes in it.**

———◆———

It is not illegal for an owner to remove the **tag** on the bottom of furniture.

English **muffins** are not English, nor are danish Danish. Those commercials telling you English muffins can bring a little bit of merry old England into your home are wrong, but so is most of television.

———◆———

There is no official def-inition of the **middle class** in the United States. Although 90 percent of the popu-

The Olympic Games have not been going on since ancient Greece. From 393 A.D. to 1896 there were no games.

lation calls itself middle class, experts say it's closer to 50 percent. So what is middle class? Some say anyone earning between $20,000 and $75,000 a year.

Roasted **peanuts** are not roasted. They are boiled in oil. Truly roasted peanuts have to be "dry roasted."

—◆—

Generally, the "rings" under one's **eyes** do not darken, or so say the medicos. They say it is the rest of the face that lightens.

The rumor that Hitler designed the Volkswagen Beetle is not completely false. He did draw the original external design of the Volkswagen. That sounds more accomplished than it really was. It was a crude sketch, but Beetles do look like it.

Conventional science says the **sperm** swims to the egg then fertilizes it. Almost everyone has seen a film showing a horde of sperm swarming about an egg until one penetrates the sphere. Well, sorry, guys, new research suggests it doesn't work that way. The sperm is not the aggressor, but rather the egg. It seems that while the sperm are wiggling about, the egg is not just passively sitting there, but rather on the hunt. And when the right sperm swims along, the egg tosses out a chemical net and snags it . . . another bastion of male supremacy dashed.

Piercing **nipples** with rings and the like is not a new punk fad. It was popular among ladies in the late 1800s.

—◆—

Most sacrificial **virgins** in ancient equatorial cultures were not forced to kill themselves. They were volunteers. The prevailing notion in such vegetation-surrounded cultures was that death fosters life, the more death, the more life for the people. It was an honored duty rather than a frightful demise, Hollywood notwithstanding.

Adam and **Eve** did not have belly buttons. . . . Think about it, and all those paintings that have got it wrong.